THE POCKET GUIDE TO

SEASONAL WALLEYE TACTICS

THE POCKET GUIDE TO
SEASONAL WALLEYE TACTICS

AN ANGLER'S QUICK REFERENCE BOOK

MONTE BURCH

Skyhorse Publishing

Skyhorse Publishing books may be purchased in bulk at special
discounts for sales promotion, corporate gifts, fund-raising, or
educational purposes. Special editions can also be created to
specifications. For details, contact the Special Sales Department,
Skyhorse Publishing, 307 West 36th Street, 11th Floor, New York,
NY 10018 or info@skyhorsepublishing.com.

Skyhorse® and Skyhorse Publishing® are registered trademarks
of Skyhorse Publishing, Inc.®, a Delaware corporation.

Visit our website at www.skyhorsepublishing.com.

10 9 8 7 6 5 4 3

Library of Congress Cataloging-in-Publication Data is available on
file.

Cover design by Tom Lau
Cover photo credit: iStockphoto.com/Vasiliy Voropaev

Print ISBN: 978-1-63450-809-4
Ebook ISBN: 978-1-63450-818-6

Printed in China

CONTENTS

INTRODUCTION

In many parts of the country walleye fishing used to be thought to be good only during the spring run and again during the early summer months. Successful walleye fishing can, however, be enjoyed year-round (in areas with open water and open seasons) by understanding the seasonal locations and habits of walleye. Granted, the habits of walleye are a bit more "mysterious" than other species such as largemouth bass, and there are times of the year when walleye are tougher to locate and catch primarily because they're roaming, following the forage. They can, however, be caught even in tough times with a little thought and effort.

The walleye fishing season can be categorized into eight major periods, although there will be some overlap between the periods. These periods are based on water temperature, fish behavior, and, most importantly, forage availability. They include: early spring, pre-spawn, spawn, post spawn, early summer, summer, fall, and winter. Walleye are found in a wide variety of locales from the North Country lakes to the southern reservoirs and from east to west. The timing of these periods will vary from area to area.

Each of the periods are described in this book along with where to find walleye in rivers, lakes, or reservoirs during the periods. Also included is specific information on best seasonal tactics including: rigs, baits, lures, and how-to with each. Again because of the wide variety of places walleye are found, some tactics may work better in some areas than others. Don't be hesitant, however, to try tactics that haven't been proven in your favorite area.

I've had the opportunity to fish with and interview some of the top walleye pros in the country, and they have also provided lots of good information that will make your walleye fishing more successful any time of the year and in almost any part of the country.

Tools

Good electronics are essential for good walleye fishing. Today's sonar units can reveal temperature, structure, baitfish, and fish as well as help you navigate.

To consistently take walleye throughout the year you'll need a few "tools" in addition to your rod, reel, and lures. First is a good temperature gauge. This can be a surface gauge such as an in-dash or an add-on unit for your boat. A handheld or electronic depth temperature gauge, however, is the best choice as these allow you to monitor temperatures at the depths walleye are most likely to inhabit, rather than just on the surface which can be quite a few degrees warmer on sunny days.

A topographical or hydrographical map of the lake, river, or reservoir you intend to fish can also be extremely valuable. It will not only indicate possible walleye-holding areas, but will also help you eliminate those areas that are not productive.

A depth finder or sonar is almost a necessity. These days sonars not only provide depth, structure, and cover information, along with baitfish and walleye locations, but also GPS, trolling speed, and mapping. Higher-end sonars also provide down- or side-finders, providing almost photographic images. Purchase the best sonar you can afford; it will make your walleye angling much more productive. Good rod holders and planer boards can also be valuable during certain periods of the year.

THE TOP FIVE WALLEYE SYSTEMS

Regardless of the time or location, five basic systems provide consistent walleye success: bottom bouncing or "rigging" live bait, jigging, slip bobbering, casting crankbaits, and trolling crankbaits. It's important to match the tactic to the conditions.

Bottom Bouncing Live Bait

Bottom bouncing live bait is a time-honored tactic. A number of variations of this rig can be used. These may consist of a standard Lindy Rig, which utilizes a walking sinker and a snelled hook, or a spinner may be added for more flash as in the Lindy Spinner Rig. Crawler harnesses are also used for this tactic. The leader from the weight to the hook can vary in length from a foot or two, to five or six feet.

Bottom bouncing a live bait or roach rig (named after Gary Roach) is a traditional and productive method.

A variety of floating devices may also be used to keep the rig just off the bottom. A wide selection of float colors as well as spinner blades are available. In a pinch a plain old egg sinker can be used to get the rig down on the bottom, with a barrel swivel behind the sinker to attach the drift rig in place.

Walking sinkers, shaped to move easily across the bottom without hanging up, are the most efficient. Even these will occasionally hang up, although they're simple and productive for even an inexperienced angler. A more sophisticated approach is the bottom-bouncing sinker. It is actually an L-shaped piece of wire with a weight on the longer bottom leg and is almost snag-free. It is fished vertically, or almost vertically as the boat drifts or is slowly trolled using a trolling motor. The point of the wire bounces along on the bottom, keeping the weight up off the bottom. If you feel the bottom, simply lift the rod tip slightly. Regardless of the style of rig or weights, live bait, including minnows, leeches, or nightcrawlers, are used with them.

The slower you can go, the more productive this system. This means either drifting with the wind or very slow trolling with a trolling motor, even back-trolling if necessary. This method will work almost all year, except when the fish are in the extreme shallows. Even deep-water walleye can be taken, although it does become harder to feel the bottom and detect strikes at those depths. Naturally the technique is a bit hard to do in areas with lots of cover such as logs, stumps, weeds, and so forth.

Jigging

Jigs are the most versatile and simplest of all lures. They can be used in many different ways and conditions, and next to live bait, have probably caught more walleye than any other lure. In fact they are often combined with live bait. A favorite tactic on Stockton Lake near my home is drifting across the flats and main lake points with a 1- to ¼-ounce Road Runner Jig tipped with a nightcrawler. This tactic can be used just about any time of the year. On Stockton, the best time of the year is

Jigs in any number of combinations of sizes and colors are, in many cases, the go-to lures for walleye.

spring/early summer when walleye move back to these areas after the post-spawn slump, from early June into midsummer. Simply follow the thermocline depth, staying just above it.

The tactic is simple and can produce quite well even for a first-timer. You can scout out these flats with a graph before fishing, although in shallow water you may spook walleye. If a flat is known to hold fish, stay off it with the motor. Motor upwind of the flat, drop the jig and worm to the bottom, then simply let the wind drift you across the flat, bouncing the jig across the bottom. It's important to stay in touch with the bottom fairly regularly, and if the wind is too fast, you may need to back-troll, or better yet slip with the wind, using just enough power to keep the boat slowly moving across the flat. A drift anchor or windsock can also be used to help slow down a drift for more effective jig fishing.

Jigs can also be used for casting for walleye and can create some exciting action early in the spring when walleye are spawning in the tributaries of lakes and reservoirs, or along traditional spawning banks. My favorite early-spring tactic is to motor upstream until stopped by an obstacle such as a dam or shoal. First step is to fish immediately below the obstacle as walleye making their spawning runs will often stop and hold just below these areas. Tailrace waters are extremely good at this time. You'll need to match the weight of the jig to the current flow and again you'll need to occasionally touch the bottom. In really fast tailrace waters many anglers use two jigs, one on a dropper about a foot above the bottom jig. This not only adds more weight, but doubles the angler's chances for a strike. Once you've thoroughly worked the water below the obstacle, move slowly downstream and cast to good walleye holding spots, such as eddies behind rocks, pockets under banks, eddy pockets on inside bends, and in and around log and drift piles, laydowns, and so forth. Jigs may be tipped with live bait, but quite often any number of plastic trailers are utilized to increase the bite.

Jigs, tipped with trailers or live bait, can also be vertically jigged to take walleye at times when nothing else seems to be working. This is particularly effective during the summer months when walleye collect in deep water off main lake points or on underwater humps. Even more effective are jigging spoons. The same type of jigging spoon used for bass, such as the Hopkins, can at times be extremely effective. Walleye pro Gary Parsons says jigging spoons are especially effective in rivers, during fall and early winter. You must match the boat speed to the current to keep your lure vertically below you. Tipping the spoon with a minnow can add to the effectiveness.

Slip Bobbering

Slip bobbering, or "controlled depth fishing" as some pro anglers call it, is a particularly effective method from late spring throughout the summer and into early fall. A tiny knot is tied around the

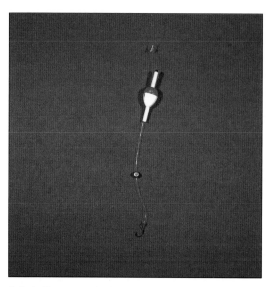

A slip bobber rig can also be productive at times.

line, or a rubber bobber stop is applied at the top of the depth you want to fish. The slip bobber has a small hole all the way through and is slid onto your line. The stop or knot is small enough to wind back on the reel as you retrieve line, while the bobber slides down the line until it reaches the bottom which is usually a split shot or two and a hook for live bait. Or you can also use a jig with or without bait. This allows you to cast quite easily, yet the baited hook or jig slides down to the depth desired, stopping when the bobber hits the knot or rubber stopper.

Slip bobbers are effective on structure such as gravel flats, rock piles, or humps in lakes or reservoirs. One particularly effective method is to look for those areas that top out with the thermocline, then fish just above that depth.

A little jigging spoon or ice-fishing spoon can also be used on a slip bobber, tipping it with a leech, crawler, or minnow. You need wind for this method to be successful. With good wave action, the slip bobber rises and falls on the waves and you can actually get jigging spoon action by letting the bobber do the work.

Sometimes walleye will get spooked off a holding place like an island or reef, especially if there is a lot of fishing pressure, and they may suspend just off the edge of the reef. Set your slip bobber to the depth they're suspended, anchor off some distance, and allow the wind to blow your bobber over the top of the fish, simply playing out line as the bobber drifts. This works especially well on a walleye chop, not really white capping, but a good strong wind. You can also use this same tactic to fish along a weed line or shoreline, if the wind is blowing parallel to the weed or shoreline.

Live Baits

All three of the tactics mentioned above involve live baits such as minnows, leeches, or nightcrawlers. Each is used in a variety of tactics and situations and each is best at certain times of the year or in specific situations.

When to Use

"We use minnows in the spring and again in the fall," says pro angler Gary Parsons. "Part of that is the convenience, they stay alive in the colder water as it holds oxygen better. I also think walleye have a preference for minnows at those times."

Crawlers are also effective in the spring and fall, but they're excellent summer bait. If they have a weak point, it's when the water temperatures are cold, mid-forties and lower, because they're less active.

Leeches are primarily summer bait, mostly because they're harder to get in the colder months, and they also stay balled up when the water is cold. One scenario where the toughness of leeches is an advantage is when the bait stealers, including drum, small smallmouth and bluegills, or perch hit the scene.

Rigging

Minnows are rigged according to the tactic used. The most common tactic for trolling, drifting, or jigging is to push the point of the hook through the lips from under the mouth where the V of the gills meet, leaving the point of the hook facing up. For trolling or drifting with a bottom bouncer, use a long-shanked hook, insert the point into the minnow's mouth and then out one of the gills. Turn the hook point and insert through the skin of the back. They'll swim upright, and as walleye have a tendency to grab a minnow through the body and not get the whole thing in their mouth, locating the hook point mid-body provides an advantage.

Minnows can also be hooked in the tail, called reverse rigging, for unusual action. This is a good tactic with floater rigs as the minnow constantly tries to swim upward and struggles like an injured baitfish. Another common method, especially for slip bobber rigging, is to hook the minnow just ahead of or behind the dorsal fin. When casting, hook through the eyes.

Leeches are almost always hooked just in front of the sucker.

The most common method of hooking nightcrawlers for walleye, regardless of the tactic, is to insert the hook or jig point through the nose. This provides the most natural appearance and action; however, walleye often short-strike worms rigged in this manner. Hooking the worm through the collar with both ends "dangling," or using a double-hook worm harness, prevents the problem. In most instances nightcrawlers are rigged whole, but sometimes small pieces of nightcrawler are best, particularly with precision vertical jigging.

Casting Crankbaits

Casting crankbaits has become extremely popular and is extremely productive in some scenarios.

Nothing works better at searching for shallow-water walleyes than casting crankbaits. Studies have shown that walleye spend a great deal more time in shallow water than most folks realize. You can cover a lot of territory in a hurry and often catch some of the biggest fish. Best times for crankbaits are early in the spring, late in the fall, and at night during the summer months. Anytime you get a wind pounding a rocky shoreline is a good time for crankbaits.

Stump beds with the roots washed out, standing and downed timber, as well as weed beds, all provide excellent cranking spots. This is akin to cranking for bass, drifting, or using a trolling motor to maneuver your boat along these areas and casting to likely spots. It's a favorite summer tactic on cover-loaded lakes such as Truman, near my home in Missouri.

Most of the traditional crankbaits, such as used for bass, will catch walleye, although a number of crankbaits are designed especially with walleye in mind. Most of these feature a tight wiggle and a slim profile, resemble shad, the most popular walleye bait, and include the jerkbaits as well as the Wally Diver by Cotton Cordell, Lindy Shadling, Berkley Flicker Shad, Strike King Walleye Elite Jerkbait, Rapala Shad Rap, and one of my favorites, the Bass Pro XPS Static Shad in shad color.

In most instances the cast should be made as close to shore or cover as possible, then start the retrieve fairly slow and speed it up as you reach deeper water. Jerkbaits should be retrieved with erratic jerks, again starting slow and speeding up as the lure reaches closer to the boat.

Trolling Crankbaits

Trolling crankbaits is also an extremely versatile and effective walleye tactic and can be one of the easiest. It is a favorite and productive tactic for walleye in my home state of Missouri. As a kid, back in the late forties, I watched relatives take good stringers of walleye from rivers such as the Osage by trolling an old Pico Perch. It was also popular to add a jig, such as a Road Runner on a leader attached to the back hook. Then I discovered the Bill

Trolling crankbaits in a variety of ways is also extremely productive.

Lewis Rat-L-Traps and the tactic quickly became red hot. Slow trolling these noise-making, lipless crankbaits has filled my livewell many, many times. Slow trolling any number of today's crankbaits, including the crankbaits mentioned for casting, as well as many others can be extremely effective.

Trolling is effective as a fish locator early in the year in rivers, in the middle of the summer in rivers when lake water warms up and forces walleye up into the cooler water, and again in late fall when walleye move up into the rivers to gorge on shad. Trolling can also be productive for locating walleye fairly fast on reservoirs and lakes as well. A good sonar is essential to locate thermocline and indicate structure as well as to locate baitfish and walleye.

Troll main lake points, islands, humps, breaklines, and other holding spots at a depth just above the thermocline in the summer months. Trolling speed will vary with the situation, but the rule of thumb is to start out slow and then add speed until you discover what the fish want. You normally need just enough speed to get the lure working properly, but not so fast the walleye don't have a chance at it. The lure should occasionally touch the bottom. Too deep and you're continually hung up—too shallow and you won't get many strikes. You will, however, hang up using this tactic. If you hang up, immediately drop the rod tip and the lure will often float back up and out from behind or under the obstacle.

Basic crankbait trolling equipment includes: a sonar unit—to visualize the bottom and to mark fish, as well as navigate and indicate trolling speed; four (or more) medium- to heavy-action, 7- to 8-foot rods; strong, abrasion-resistant line; an arsenal of crankbaits that run at various depths; four or more rod holders, planer boards, and snap weights of various sizes.

The biggest mistake anglers make when trolling for walleye is failing to test lures to determine the speed at which they are most effective and the approximate depth at which they run. Many crankbait manufacturers list the depth their lures will attain. Three primary elements affect how a lure runs through the water when it's trolled: line diameter, speed of the troll, and the distance a lure is positioned from the boat.

To test lure capabilities, place the same size line on all rods and position all lures an equal distance from the boat. Then vary trolling speeds to see how each lure reacts. Note the lure action created and the depth the lure runs at different speeds. Also pay attention to how lures run through the water. Natural presentation is important. Crankbaits that veer left or right cost you fish. Tune lures when necessary. Trolling puts a lot of punishment on the line, so respool frequently with abrasion-resistant line, such as Offshore Angler MAGIBRAID Trolling line. Extremely light, braided line trolls deeper than monofilament. Constantly check hooks and make sure they're extremely sharp. Constant contact with rocks and other structures quickly dulls hooks.

Begin using lures that run at different depths until you pinpoint where the walleye are holding. When you determine the pattern, change to the lures that run at and above the depth the fish are located. Experiment with different baits and cull out ineffective lures. Walleye change their patterns during the day. If the action slows, make some changes. For instance, switch from straight-running crankbaits to wobbling lures.

Longer rods and planer boards can also be used to widen the expanse of water covered, and move lures away from the boat. Planer boards are especially useful for reaching fish that are spooky or are holding in shallow water along shorelines.

Crankbaits can be long-lined (without weights) or use snap weights when trolling open water to quickly increase depth. Line counter reels can also be used to position the crankbait the same distance from the boat each time. Lead-core trolling is also a popular tactic. Once used primarily for deep-water trolling, walleye anglers are now using short, four- and five-foot, lead core leaders for more shallow water. Regardless, lead core trolling allows cranks to run at a higher speed. Run at five miles an hour, the larger diameter of lead core actually helps lift the lure—the opposite of what you would think. Other means

RIVERS

PERIOD	TEMP	LOCATION	TACTIC
EARLY SPRING	32-39 DEGREES F.	DEEP HOLES AND BELOW DAMS ON RIVERS. BEHIND WING DAMS, ROCKS, LOG PILES, OR ANYTHING THAT BREAKS UP CURRENT AND CREATES AN EDDY IN LARGER RIVERS.	SMALL 1/8 TO 1/4 OZ. JIG TIPPED WITH MINNOW AND FISHED VERTICALLY VERY, VERY SLOW. OR USE TINY JIGS ALONE, CASTING FROM THE BANKS OR FISHED VERTICALLY JUST OFF THE BOTTOM.
PRE-SPAWN	40-44 DEGREES F.	IN RIVERS, BELOW SHOALS· AND IN TAILRACE WATER BELOW DAMS. IN RESERVOIRS ALONG RIPRAP OF DAMS AND BRIDGE OR ROAD CAUSEWAYS, AND OFF ROCKY POINTS.	IN RIVERS, TROLLING CRANKBAITS THROUGH CENTER OF RIVER, CASTING JIGS TO COVER. IN RESERVOIRS CASTING JIGS OR JERK BAITS AT NIGHT, TROLLING DURING DAYTIME WITH CRANKBAITS.
SPAWN	45-50 DEGREES F.	IN RIVERS SHALLOW SHOALS, AND IN TRIBUTARIES. IN LAKES WINDY POINTS, HUMPS AND SUNKEN ISLANDS. IN RESERVOIRS RIPRAP OF DAMS AND BRIDGES.	IN RIVERS TINY JIGS CAST TO THE AREAS. IN LAKES AND RESERVOIRS MINNOW AND BOTTOM WALKING SINKER, OR CRANKBAITS OR STICKBAITS CAST TO THE AREA.
POST SPAWN	50-60 DEGREES F.	NEAR SPAWNING AREAS OR ON MIGRATORY ROUTES BETWEEN SHALLOW SPAWNING AREAS AND DEEP WATER.	SMALL JIGS CAST OR SMALL CRANKBAITS CAST OR TROLLED. JIGS TIPPED WITH NIGHT CRAWLERS. CONTOUR FISHING WITH BOTTOM BOUNCER AND MINNOW RIG.

LAKES & RESERVOIRS

PERIOD	TEMP	LOCATION	TACTIC
EARLY SUMMER	60-75 DEGREES F.	SHALLOW MUD FLATS NEXT TO DEEP WATER CHANNELS, AND JUST OFF RIPRAP IN RESERVOIRS. LONG MAIN LAKE POINTS IN LAKES AND RESERVOIRS. BACK UP INTO MAJOR TRIBUTARIES.	DRIFTING ACROSS FLATS WITH JIG TIPPED WITH NIGHT CRAWLER, OR USE BOTTOM BOUNCING RIG. TROLL POINTS WITH CRANKBAITS.
LATE SUMMER	75-80 DEGREES F.	MAIN LAKE POINTS IN LAKES AND RESERVOIRS. DEEPER HOLES IN RIVERS.	FOLLOW CONTOURS WITH JIG AND NIGHT CRAWLER OR BOTTOM BOUNCING RIG WITH NIGHT CRAWLER. USE SLIP BOBBER AND HOOK WITH WEIGHT AND NIGHT CRAWLER OR LEECH.
FALL	60-55 DEGREES F.	SHALLOW IN FLATS ALONG RIPRAP AND ROCKY BANKS IN LAKES AND RESERVOIRS. IN LARGE HOLES OF MAJOR TRIBUTARIES.	TROLLING AREAS WITH CRANKBAITS, DRIFTING WITH LIVE BAIT RIGS OR CASTING CRANKBAITS TO SHALLOWS. SPOON JIGGING TO SCHOOLS OF FISH.
WINTER	32-38 DEGREES F.	DEEP HOLES IN MAJOR TRIBUTARIES, WASH-OUT HOLES BELOW DAMS AND LOCK AND DAMS SYSTEMS.	VERTICAL JIGGING WITH LIVE BAIT ON JIG. SMALL JIGGING SPOONS CAN ALSO BE VERTICALLY JIGGED.

of getting the lures deeper include diving planer boards.

The remainder of this book contains seasonal information, and begins with a quick reference chart with the information condensed and available for instant use.

EARLY SPRING

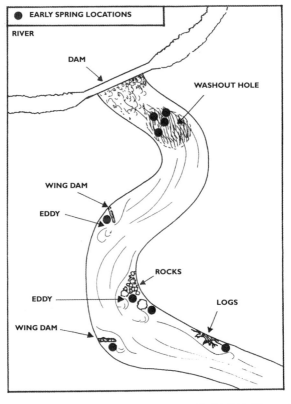

Water Temperature: 32 to 39 degrees F

Although many anglers don't start fishing for walleye until the first "news" of the walleye run, the best fishing often occurs in January or February to early March, depending on ice out, geographical locale, or local fishing regulations. Granted, the weather is totally unpredictable—as is the fishing. It is, however, a time of the year when numbers of trophy walleye can be caught.

Regardless of north or south, east or west, rivers are the best bet for early season walleye. In the north the best fishing is often before the snow starts melting (in areas with open seasons). When that happens, the water starts rising, mud and silt starts dirtying up the rivers, and fishing slows down.

"One of the reasons for good success in early spring is the majority of the walleye migrate back up into the rivers and tributaries in the fall," says walleye pro Ralph Brunner of Manitowoc, Wisconsin. "They'll often stay all winter and by early spring you have a tremendous concentration of fish in certain areas of the rivers.

"Even if lakes are still iced in, the rivers can provide good fishing. As long as you can find a place to slide a boat in and use a little common sense in boating safety, you'll find a place for walleye fishing."

Major rivers are best. If a dam is generating power, or the river is a navigation river, it will be open all winter. Incidentally, these same areas are major fishing spots for sauger, a walleye cousin.

Places that don't have a lot of current, such as eddies and wing dams are key spots. Since the water is extremely cold, the fish really don't like to fight a lot of

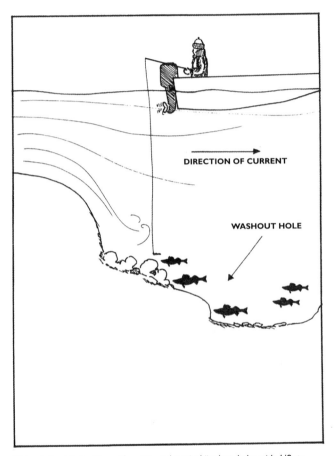

Maintain boat in position with motor and vertical jig deep holes with 1/8- to 3/8-ounce jig tipped with minnow.

current. They'll be lying tight behind a rock, snugged up against a fallen tree or really hugging close to the bottom, and sometimes quite close to the shore. In fact, at this time of the year they can be as shallow as two to three feet.

Washout holes, or the deep water holes just below dams or wing dams caused by the constant current, are prime spots. These may be found a few feet or several hundred yards below the dam. Early in the year concentrations of big walleye can be found in these areas. As the water temperature starts moving up, so do the fish. However, they usually won't come out of these deep-water holes until the water temperature reaches 40 to 44 degrees.

Lure Choices

"The number one bait is a jig tipped with a minnow," says Ralph. "Because of the water clarity, 4- to 6-pound test line is required."

A jig is the number one lure of choice.

The weight of the jig will depend on how much current and how deep the water is you're fishing, usually ranging from ⅛- to ⅜-ounce. Regardless, work the bait as slow as possible.

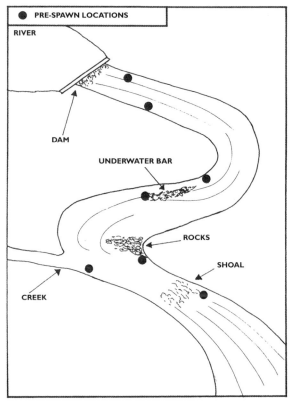

● PRE-SPAWN LOCATIONS

RIVER

DAM

UNDERWATER BAR

ROCKS

SHOAL

CREEK

Water Temperature: 40 to 44 degrees F

As the days lengthen and the water temperature slowly rises, walleye fishing continues to get better. Watch your water temperature gauge.

Many reservoirs and some lakes have both river and lake spawning walleye. Basically the tactics for catching both are similar, you just look for walleye in different spots.

Some river-spawning walleye spend a portion of the year in the main body of the reservoir. They migrate upstream either late in the fall, in the winter, or very early spring.

Other walleye spend their entire lives in rivers, moving up and down the river into shallow and deep-water holes dictated by the seasons, water fluctuation, location of forage, and water temperature.

Although some walleye have been upstream since fall, a mass upstream migration occurs very early in the spring as river-run walleye look for shoals and riffles to spawn. Typically the walleye move upstream until they reach extremely shallow water, the right spawning habitat (which is usually traditional), or an obstruction such as a dam that prevents further travel. For that reason the areas below dams often provide some of the best early season walleye fishing when the fish become concentrated in these small areas.

On smaller rivers and in many tailrace waters, early season walleye fishing is often a bank fishing affair. It's a matter of casting small jigs into eddies of tailrace waters or into the holes just below riffles.

Another tactic I've found extremely effective for early season river walleye is slow trolling upstream until I'm stopped by shallow water or obstacles.

Then drift back downstream, using the trolling motor to keep the boat aligned properly, and casting tiny jigs to pockets, eddies, log jams, and other areas along the banks of the river. This tactic can be deadly for finding scattered, early season river walleye, but it must be done super, super slow. Tipping the jig with a minnow can increase chances for success.

Walleye are basically bottom huggers, and trolled lures must get down close to the bottom, yet not continually hang up. Big lipped deep-diving crankbaits are not the answer for most river trolling conditions as they usually dig too deep. The best crankbaits are the noise-making vibrators such as the Bill Lewis Rat-L-Trap, Cordell Rattlin' Spot, Storm Texas Shad, and Whopper Stopper Bayou Boogie. Color should be white or chrome with red, black, or blue markings. Occasionally chartreuse will produce. One-half ounce is the best size choice for most conditions, but in fast or deep water, a ¾-ounce lure will get deeper and can produce some monster-size walleye.

Line size should be 8- to 10-pound test on either a good quality bait casting or spinning outfit. Braided line is an extremely good choice. A medium weight, long rod with a fairly limber tip provides more action to the trolled lure than a short stiff rod.

Basically this is "long line" trolling with about 30 to 50 yards of line out, depending on water depth. The lure should ride just off the bottom. If you occasionally feel the "tick" of the lure striking the bottom, you're trolling just about the right speed and/or have out the right amount of line. If you don't feel the bottom or continually hang up, you're trolling too fast or too slow. Regardless of your best efforts, you're still going to occasionally hang up.

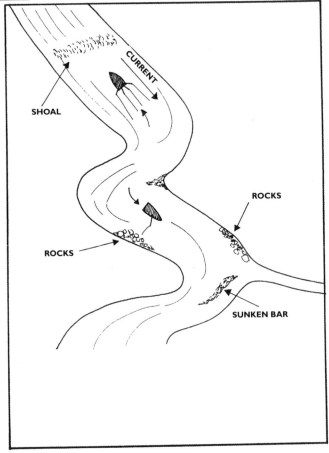

Slowly troll upstream with shallow running crankbaits. Then drift back downstream casting tiny jigs to the cover.

Reservoir spawning walleye congregate along the rocky points, riprap dams, and the riprap road causeways, with the smaller males first, then the bigger females not far behind. Although the fish won't be aggressively feeding, there will be large concentrations of them.

Casting marabou jigs is the best tactic at this time. If the weather is calm, a boat can be used. In many prime walleye holding spots on reservoirs and lakes, early spring

Night fishing is an effective method at this time of the year.

winds can be ferocious and casting from the bank is sometimes the only option, unless your boat is equipped to deal with high waves and you have the expertise to handle the boat.

Night fishing off the face of reservoir dams and riprap bridges and causeways is extremely effective at this time of the year. Walleye are spooky, light-sensitive fish, often staying in deeper water during daylight hours but moving into shallow water at night. Shallow running crankbaits such as Rat-L-Traps and minnow or jerkbaits such as Rapalas, Rogues, Wally Diver, or Shadling are especially effective. A careful wader can have extremely good luck with this tactic during the early season. Wear plenty of clothes, a good pair of insulated chest waders, a life jacket, and use only a small penlight to tie on lures. A flashlight beam cast around the water surface will quickly spook fish back out of shallow water.

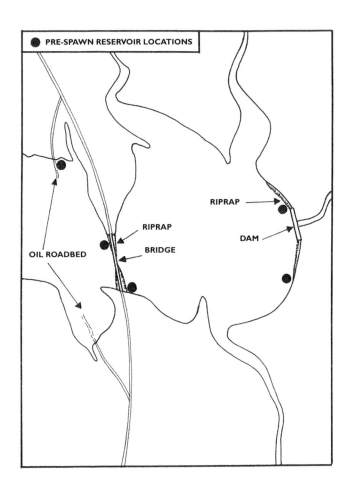

PRE-SPAWN RESERVOIR LOCATIONS

RIPRAP

RIPRAP

DAM

OIL ROADBED

BRIDGE

Trolling can also be effective. Start at the deeper depths of riprap dams and bridge causeways, trolling first with shallow water crankbaits. Continue trolling and gradually move in shallower until you can cast to the bank with the lightweight jigs.

"Any time you have wind pounding into a shoreline is a good time to cast crankbaits," says pro walleye angler Mike McClelland of Pierre, South Dakota. "Just toss into the shallows next to the bank and retrieve starting slow and gaining speed as you reach deeper water."

A number of different rigs can be productive for early season walleye, depending on the situation. However, five basic rigs and tactics can be used a majority of the time.

1. Riprap tailrace or lake casting rig consists of a small ⅛- to ¹⁄₁₆-ounce jig tied to the end of the line and a small

dropper jig, usually of a different color, tied about eighteen inches above. Rig is cast into eddies, pockets, and rip-rap of tailrace waters below dams or along dam facings.

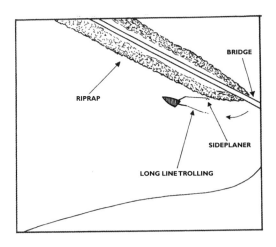

2. River or lake casting rig consists of single small ⅛- to 1⁄16-ounce jig, preferably with a spinner blade attached such as the Road Runner.

3. River bottom bouncer drift trolling rig is bottom-bouncing weight rig of stainless steel wire with keel-type weight added. Can be used with Lindy rig or jig-tipped with minnow or nightcrawler.

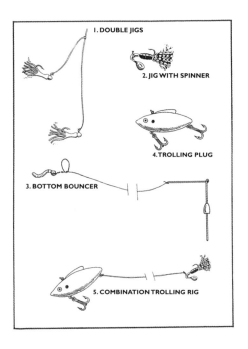

1. DOUBLE JIGS

2. JIG WITH SPINNER

4. TROLLING PLUG

3. BOTTOM BOUNCER

5. COMBINATION TROLLING RIG

4. River plug trolling rig is a noisemaker vibrator plug with hooks bent inward slightly with needle nose pliers to help prevent hangups.

5. Combination trolling rig is a vibrator lure with small jig tied on 18-inch leader. Good on lake or river.

SPAWNING

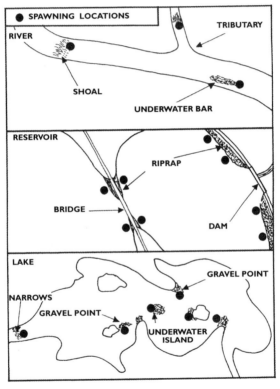

SPAWNING LOCATIONS

RIVER

TRIBUTARY

SHOAL

UNDERWATER BAR

RESERVOIR

RIPRAP

BRIDGE

DAM

LAKE

GRAVEL POINT

NARROWS

GRAVEL POINT

UNDERWATER ISLAND

Water Temperature: 45 to 50 degrees F

During the actual spawn, which may last from a few days to weeks, fishing usually drops off. Walleye spawn in fairly shallow water of one to eight feet in traditional spots with small gravel or rubble bottoms that are clean of mud, silt, and weeds, and with some current. Normally you'll catch only the smaller males during the spawn

Jerkbaits retrieved slowly just under the surface at night can be deadly.

and thankfully not all walleye spawn at the same time. If you do, however, catch females laden with eggs, release them carefully back into the water.

In rivers, look for shallow shoals of the main river and tributaries. Obstacles such as dams may stop upstream spawning runs and concentrate fish. In lakes, look for windswept points, humps, and sunken islands with rubble and gravel. In reservoirs the same structure may attract spawning walleye, as will riprap along dams and bridge causeways.

During the daytime, use small jigs tipped with a minnow. If night fishing is allowed, again tiny jigs cast to these areas can produce. A minnow and walking sinker can also be productive at times. Stickbaits and jerkbaits retrieved slowly just under the surface can be productive as can small shallow to medium running crankbaits cranked down slowly just off the bottom.

POST SPAWN

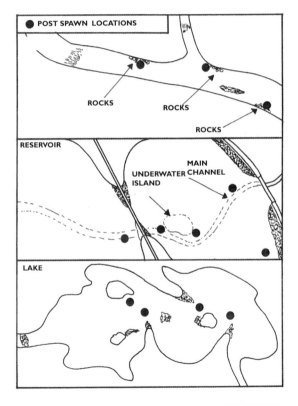

POST SPAWN LOCATIONS

ROCKS

ROCKS

ROCKS

RESERVOIR

MAIN CHANNEL

UNDERWATER ISLAND

LAKE

Water Temperature: 50 to 60 degrees F

Once the peak of the spawn is over, old marble eyes drifts back down from the shallow spawning grounds of river shoals or reservoir riprap and goes into a two- to three-week deep-water seclusion. Walleye can be caught at that time, but they're scattered and fishing can be tough. After this short interim of relative inactivity, walleye then move back up to traditional early summer shallow water feeding areas and go on a feeding binge that may last through June into July.

In order to successfully fish this transition period, we need to break it down into two different categories. Early post spawn and late post spawn, or the resting period. Walleye are found in different areas for each of these periods and each requires somewhat different tactics.

During the early post-spawn period, primary catches will consist of one- to three-pound males. They are the first to move onto the spawning grounds and the first to leave. Best spots to fish after the peak of the spawn are relatively shallow areas near the spawning grounds and along a migration route to deeper water. They're fairly aggressive at this time; however, you won't be able to consistently catch the bigger females during this period. The best times to fish during this period are during low light levels such as on overcast, dark days, windy days, and early in the morning or late in the evening.

Jigs such as the Road Runner are excellent choices at this time, but slow down your retrieve as post-spawn walleye are not as fast at picking up the bait as pre-spawn and spawning fish. Small crankbaits resembling minnows can also be used with some success. Probably the best tactic

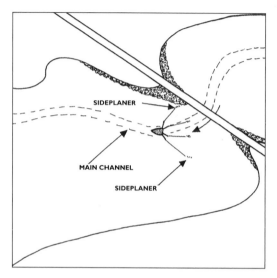

Troll near to spawning areas and migratory routes between spawning areas and deep water with small plugs. Sideplaners can widen trolling pattern to cover more area.

is to troll the areas adjacent to spawning grounds and nearby deep water holes. Use planer boards to spread out lines and cover more water.

The last part of the post season is dismal. There's absolutely no other way to describe it. Although the males have been moving gradually to deeper water, the females move much faster once they decide to leave the spawning grounds, and what was a good producing area during spawn and early post spawn is now barren. Walleye can be caught during this bleak period but first you have to find them and

Bottom bouncer rig with spinner and nightcrawler or minnow is used; following the contour, walleye are located with sonar and trolling motor.

they tend to be more scattered than during the other two portions of the post-spawn period. A good sonar is almost a must to be able to pinpoint fish at this time. Walleye also tend to be even more finicky about taking lures or bait than at any other time.

Use the lightest line and the smallest jigs and tip them with nightcrawlers or small minnows. Drift over deep holes adjacent to spawning grounds to catch an occasional fish or two. Even if you do luck into fish, this will usually only result in one from each spot, picking up one here, another there, and so forth. The pick-up will often be very light, almost unnoticeable so you really have to be on your toes for any difference in the feel of the line.

Walleye still have to eat, however, and one good method of prospecting a lot of deep water is to use a bottom bouncer weight to keep your jig and minnow or rig and minnow continually bouncing on the bottom. Watch your sonar and using your trolling motor, follow the contour where most fish are located, raising or lowering the bottom-bouncing weight rig to match the structure contour.

EARLY SUMMER

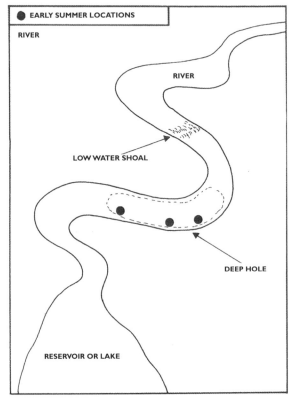

EARLY SUMMER LOCATIONS

RIVER

RIVER

LOW WATER SHOAL

DEEP HOLE

RESERVOIR OR LAKE

Water Temperature: 60 to 75 degrees F

After the thankfully brief post-spawn period comes early summer, a time when walleye start to regroup and move on to their favorite summertime shallow-water haunts. This begins with a feeding binge when walleye move onto the shallow mud

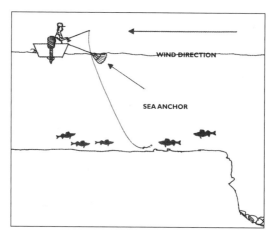

Use trolling motor, sea anchor, drift sock, or Power Paddles to create controlled drift across flats. Jig with nightcrawler is fished just off the bottom.

flats, the riprap of roads, bridges, or dams, as well as on long main lake points and back up into deeper holes of the main tributaries of many reservoirs. Walleye and sauger will both congregate in certain areas usually where a mud bottom changes to rock.

Several methods are effective depending on the type of structure, water depth, and clarity. Drifting mud flats is a top producer. First look for areas with seven to eight feet of water and a rock or hard clay bottom next to deep water. Slowly graphing flats will usually reveal schools of fish. Don't throw out your anchor or fire up the trolling motor and start fishing. Walleye on these flats can be very spooky. The best tactic is to motor clear of the flat or stay off it completely with the motor. Instead, motor upwind and then drift across the flat using your graph

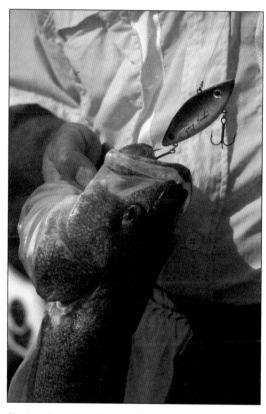

Slow, long-line trolling with crankbaits is an excellent tactic at this time.

and a jig, such as a Road Runner tipped with a nightcrawler.

If you already know the location of the flat, throw out a buoy close but not on top of the fish. Then motor upwind and drift back across the flat.

The bottom-bouncing rig is an excellent method for getting your bait down on the bottom for this drifting tactic. Add a spinner rig with a nightcrawler and you're in business. The most successful days are when a wind is kicking a chop on the water. Quite often you will drift too fast for effective fishing on those days. You can slow down your boat by dragging a sea anchor, which is nothing more than a big canvas bucket. Two sea anchors provide even more control. The new electronic "power paddles" can be used even more effectively.

When walleye are concentrated on the points instead of flats, trolling with Wiggle Warts or Rat-L-Traps in either silver or

Many walleye will also move back up into rivers due to increased oxygen and lower temperatures.

black is the best tactic. Again, locating fish with electronics is best, although a slow trolling sweep with crankbaits is the old-time fish locator. Adjust trolling depth and speed until you get lucky, then match the situation for consistent results. Unless you're occasionally ticking the bottom with your lure, you aren't going to have much success trolling for walleye. You may have to add weight to your lure to get it down or simply use bigger lures. Some of my best catches have been on the big ¾-ounce Rat-L-Trap in Smokey Joe color.

This is also the best tactic for walleye that have moved back into tributaries or

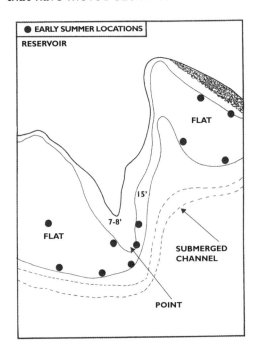

● EARLY SUMMER LOCATIONS

RESERVOIR

FLAT

15'

7-8'

FLAT

SUBMERGED
CHANNEL

POINT

streams. Many walleye actually don't leave their river habitat, they merely drop into the deeper holes during the mid post-spawn period, then move back upstream into shallower water holes for the early summer feeding binge.

I have found, however, that river walleye as a whole do not have as consistent a pattern as do their reservoir cousins. They can be found in one location one day and for no reason vanish only to be found several miles away in another hole the next day. Two or three days later they may be back to the original hole.

Other tactics can also be effective at this time of the year. If you can find walleye schooled up, try vertical jigging right over top of them. Get on the river or creek channel where there's 15 to 18 feet of water and run a sonar over the area—you'll often find schools of fish. A jigging spoon can be productive, as can a Road

Runner or a jig and grub. Best color is smoke or clear with added sparkle.

If you're running up in the rivers and creeks early in the morning or late in the evening when walleye are up close to the bank, a Wiggle Wart, Shad Rap, Rat-L-Trap, Wally Diver, or similar crankbaits can also be productive.

LATE SUMMER

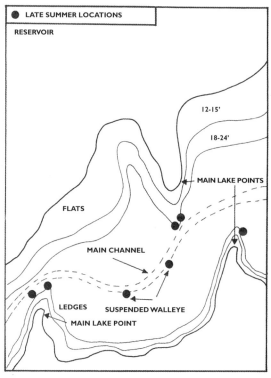

LATE SUMMER LOCATIONS

RESERVOIR

12-15'

18-24'

MAIN LAKE POINTS

FLATS

MAIN CHANNEL

SUSPENDED WALLEYE

LEDGES

MAIN LAKE POINT

Water Temperature: 75 to 80 degrees F

During the heat of the summer months use a sonar to locate walleye on the main points in the heat of the day. Always go over these areas in idle. Once you spot walleye, throw out a marker, but not directly over the fish or you'll spook them. These fish are usually 18 to 24 feet deep or deeper. Use a Road Runner jig with all the dressing pulled off, tip it with a nightcrawler, and add one split shot about 15 to 18 inches above the jig. Drop the jig all the way to the bottom, then pick it up about a foot off the bottom. Use your trolling motor at the slowest speed and troll around as slow as possible dragging the worm.

A big minnow can also be used. Hook it through the top of the nose and out the bottom so the minnow rides upside down. He will continually try to turn over creating more action.

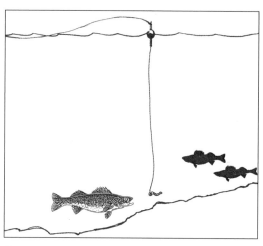

Slip bobber set so bait is just off the bottom is used to fish points and flats. Use 1 to 1/0 hook and nightcrawler with just enough weight to get to the bottom.

Work these points back and forth, checking the areas where the river channels come up and touch the points.

During the summer when walleye are located primarily on the main lake points or underwater bumps or reefs of both natural lakes and man-made reservoirs, slip bobbering is also effective. After locating walleye, set the slip bobber to hold your bait at the proper depth. Anchor off to one side of the walleye and either toss the bobber over top of them or drift using your trolling motor.

"Another tactic is to pick the points on the windy side of the reservoir with the roughest water," says pro Mike Theyerl from Two Rivers, Wisconsin. "This wind tends to create a mudline along the points that concentrates the walleye. If the water is calm, fish the flats next to the main submerged river channel, drifting the areas and concentrating on the old original channel. A vertical jigging tactic is used. Early on use minnows, switching to leeches or nightcrawlers after the water warms up."

This period lasts until heat, light, and forage cause walleye to start moving into deeper summer haunts.

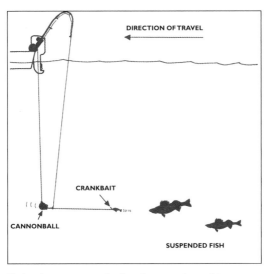

DIRECTION OF TRAVEL

CRANKBAIT

CANNONBALL

SUSPENDED FISH

During the summer months, downriggers can be used to run crankbaits or live bait at the depths needed to reach suspended deep-water walleye.

Walleye will suspend in some lakes during the hot summer months and they may be down as deep as 40, 50, 60, or even 100 feet. This is much too deep for crankbaits, so the logical choice is downriggers. Although primarily popular on the Great

Lakes, downriggers are becoming popular almost everywhere and can be used quite successfully to take suspended summer walleye. Downriggers are also available in a wide range of sizes and prices to fit almost any boat. After graphing and locating walleye, or more specifically the depth they're suspending, set the downriggers for that depth and slow troll through the schools. Match the lure choice to the forage. In most instances, long minnow imitation lures, such as the Shad Rap, Rapala, Rattling Shiner from Bass Pro, Rebel, Rattlin' Rouge, Shadling, Wally Diver, Rat-L-Trap, Bomber, Storm Thinfin, and Ratt'L Spot Minnow are the best for lakes with smelt and shad, although small spoons such as Little Cleo, Cabela's Canadian Spoons, Krocodile, and Dardevle can also be productive for shad-based lakes.

Black and silver or black and gold are good color choices for crankbaits, while silver with orange, red, or green can be good in spoons. In stained water use orange or fluorescent green. Live bait, such as a minnow, behind spinner rigs can also be effective although more work.

Fall is an excellent time to catch a stringer of big walleye.

Water Temperature: 60 to 55 degrees F

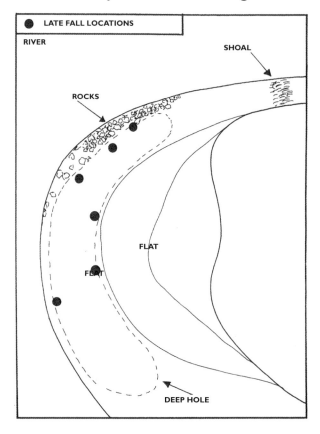

LATE FALL LOCATIONS

RIVER

SHOAL

ROCKS

FLAT

FLAT

DEEP HOLE

Early in the fall as cooling weather and the usual rains bring an influx of water, walleye again start moving shallow in reservoirs and lakes. It's another dandy time to fish these areas, as well as below the dams in the tailrace areas. Small, Road Runner-type jigs are top choices. White or yellow patterns can't be beat in the jigs for enticing old marble eyes to take a swipe. They can also be used with light line, which is a necessity for the sneaky attack needed for wary walleye. Use nothing larger than 10-pound test and go as light as you possibly can depending on the situation. Braided line is an excellent choice. A long, light-action rod can also be of advantage.

Fall and early winter months are quite often overlooked by most anglers as prime-time walleye periods. In addition, many anglers have discovered that these months are extremely productive and are keeping it a secret. The fall and early winter months are, in fact, a "hot" season for walleye for several reasons. During the summer most lakes stratify into three separate layers depending on the temperature. The top portion of the lake is warmer and has the most oxygen. The bottom portion is colder and usually devoid of oxygen. A third layer lies between the two and is called the thermocline. During the summer months, walleye will often be concentrated on the flats and points just off the deeper water of the creek or main river channels in a manmade lake. Depth will depend mostly on the thermocline, with the fish holding just above or right down on the thermocline.

Then in late summer/early fall, the water surface begins to cool down and combined with wind, creates a turnover of the lake, mixing the water layers. This also tends to scatter walleye over a greater area. Fish will not only be spread over a greater amount of water, but at varying depths as well. It's tougher to pattern late season walleye for that reason, and why many late season walleye are lucky catches by bass anglers. Immediately after the turnover, fishing success usually drops drastically because the fish are disoriented and a pattern has not yet been established. This period may last only a few days, a week, or more.

After this period, walleye usually move into a more aggressive feeding activity as they get ready for winter. Females will be starting to carry eggs and with the summer crop of forage, a general feeding binge begins. In addition to the cooling water, there is usually more weather activity, a rise in water level, and all the things that in general offer the best conditions for walleye fishing.

Previously the best fishing was during evening, night, and morning hours in the hot weather, however, any time of the day can be good in late fall/early winter. The water temperature will usually be in the mid to low 50s at this time but as it drops into the 40s, walleye will again start to bunch up and congregate in specific winter holding spots where they will stay until the beginning of their spring spawning movement. Find one of these spots and you'll be in hawg heaven. Key areas again will be rocky ledges, underwater

Troll with medium to shallow running plugs. Hooks can be bent inwards to prevent excessive hangups.

humps and islands, and along the riprap of bridge and road causeways and dams. Graphing these areas is an easy and productive method of locating schooling fish. Or you can simply troll these areas until you hang a fish and then concentrate on the areas where the fish was taken.

Best lures for trolling are the minnow imitators; a silver or white Wiggle Wart, Rat-L-Trap, Rebel Double Deep Wee-R, Cordell Rattlin' Spot, Tom Mann Shad-Mann, Rapala Shad Rap, Model A Bomber, Bagley Diving B III, and Whopper Stopper Shadrak.

Once you locate a cluster, you might try some spoon jigging. Popular with largemouth, hybrid, and striper fishermen for years, it's catching on fast in my part of the country for walleye when they're congregated, such as during the early winter months.

Another popular tactic is to fish with a jig and minnow combination, with large

Jigging spoon should be fished vertically. Drop to bottom, sweep rod tip up about 2 feet, drop jig with control on line to feel strikes.

minnows the choice in the fall months as they more closely match the size of the forage.

In fall, walleye fishing success increases on the rivers as well as the lakes. In fact, my favorite fall walleye water is a river. The larger rivers usually offer the best chances for success at this time. Since rivers don't stratify as lakes do, they offer more consistent year-round walleye fishing although again the fall months are usually more productive than hot-weather months. The key to river fishing is finding the fish, the major factor in any kind of lake or river fishing. While walleye in lakes tend to scatter during the fall flush, they usually congregate earlier in rivers. This makes it appear that finding fish is tougher until you understand that particular areas attract fall walleye.

Most good walleye rivers consist of stretches of gradual gradient with medium current (at normal conditions) for several miles followed by a deep water pool below shoals or in bends. Once the water temperature drops into the low forties, walleye will start congregating in the holes or deep water bends that offer just the right amount of current, depth, safety, and food. These fish will be confined to a very small area and finding them is tough. Again, a good graph can be invaluable in screening top walleye holes. You can also narrow your search down by looking for structure that walleye like. Walleye prefer a flat or series of flats located on river bends. If you can find a bend that has a deep scoured hole, a good length of normal river, and a wide flat edging out into these deep water holes, you'll be looking at a prime spot for congregating winter walleye.

Where walleye are located in respect to the structure will often dictate whether or not they are active or passive and easy or tough to catch.

This doesn't necessarily mean you can't catch passive fish or that active feeders are easy, but you do need a more precise presentation for passive fish. In most instances fish located deep in the structure and holding tight into eddies will be passive.

You can still catch them but the lure has to pass almost in front of their nose, and the slower the lure moves, the better the chance for success. Fish located on the edge of the breaks between the flats and deep water holes are usually coming off a passive or active feeding period and again precise presentation in speed and lure position are important. Fish spread out over the flat are usually actively feeding and the easiest to catch. Even a lure that is too fast or misses the fish a foot or so will often be grabbed. Normally walleye will move up and down from the hole onto the flat and from passive to active feeding periods throughout the day. Being there when they're feeding can result in amazing success while a frustrating time can be spent fishing and watching inactive fish ignore your best offerings.

The best choices in lures and tactics varies from locale to locale, but trolling is the number one producer in most instances. Deep running crankbaits that nick or tick the bottom are excellent choices. Start trolling across the flat, then the edge of the structure break, and finally deep water holes.

Gary Parsons of Chilton, Wisconsin, likes to spoon jig this time of the year, matching the boat speed to the current and vertically jigging. The spoons are tipped with minnows.

WINTER

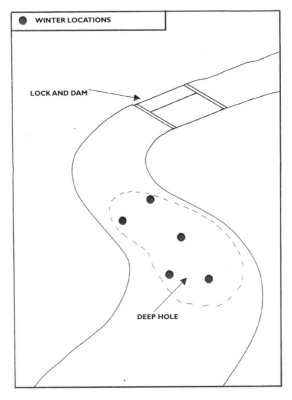

WINTER LOCATIONS

LOCK AND DAM

DEEP HOLE

Water Temperature: 32 to 38 degrees F

As with very early spring, the best fishing will be in the rivers. Tailrace waters below some dams can provide walleye fishing throughout the winter, although

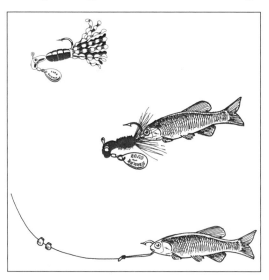

Jig or jig tipped with live bait or simply a minnow with hook and just enough weight to keep it down are top winter walleye producers.

it may be spotty at best. Other good choices are on the larger, navigable rivers, fishing the pools between locks and dams. As in very early spring, walleye will be located in the deepest holes nearest an upstream obstruction such as a dam. Although some walleye will move into these areas in fall, even more move up in the winter months in anticipation of the spring spawn. The major deep holes are the most productive.

Fishing below locks and dams is one of the most popular wintertime tactics.

In some instances bank fishing with jigs can produce. Size depends on the current and ranges from ⅛ to ⅜ ounce. Boating over the holes and vertical jigging is, however, the single most productive method. A graph or LCR makes the chore of locating the holes and walleye, as well as staying over them, much easier. Boat control is a must. Dressing the jig with a live minnow will increase productivity. Small jigging spoons can also be effective at this time of the year, again used vertically. A live bait rig can also be used and consists of a number one to 1/0 hook, a 3- to 4-inch shiner, and just enough weight to get the lure down.

GETTING AND KEEPING LIVE BAITS

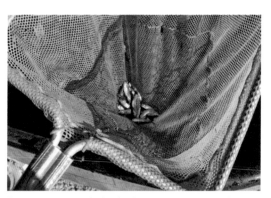

Keeping minnows and other live baits can provide baits when you need them.

You got up well before dawn and drove for a couple of hours to your favorite lake only to discover the bait shop hadn't opened yet. Your buddy told you the night before the walleye were hitting good on minnows, but you don't have any and you're anxious to get on the water. After an hour of frustrating waiting, the bait shop finally opens. Has this happened to you? It has to me more than once.

Although many different artificial baits are great walleye lures, oftentimes the best bet is live bait. Depending on the season and forage factors, this can include minnows, nightcrawlers, or leeches. Having the bait you need at the right time is an important facet of walleye angling, and keeping bait can be even more invaluable.

Minnows

Minnows are often the best choice for coldwater walleye, but not just any minnow may be effective. Depending on locale, walleye may show a preference to specific minnow species. Fathead minnows are the hardiest and will normally stay lively longer than the chubs or shiners. You may, however, be limited to what you can purchase in your local area. You can also use a minnow trap or even a seine to acquire minnows, if you have access to a small creek. For the most part, however, these will be chubs or shiners.

Regardless of how you get them, minnows left at the end of the day can present a problem, as can getting minnows early in the morning. Serious minnow dunkers go through a good amount of bait in a season's time. Keeping minnows at home can cut down on the cost and provide a

Minnows, crawfish, and other live baits can often by trapped with a minnow trap.

reliable supply of bait when you want it. Many products are now available, including tanks, aerators, and water treatment chemicals, that aid in keeping minnows frisky and healthy. You can keep a limited number of minnows alive with a DC- or battery-powered aerator, and some aerator units can be placed in any container. A big insulated cooler makes a good "minnow tank." A 110V-system can also be set up to keep bait indefinitely. A number

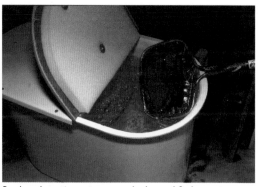

Purchased aerating systems can also be used for home storage of baits.

of aerators for use in tanks are available, as are tanks and/or complete units. The electric supply must be protected by a ground-fault interrupter.

My system consists of a Rubbermaid 60-gallon stock tank with a 110V-aerator. This is a quite simple system, but it can also be improved with a bit of effort. In order to support the agitator and also to keep the bait quiet and prevent algae growth from light, make a lid of ⅜-inch

An aerated bait tank can be used to hold any number of live baits. The tank shown utilizes 110V-aerator with a plastic stock tank

treated plywood, with a hinged lift-up section. Actually the lid is in three sections, and I divided the tank in half to keep minnows of two different sizes. A piece of treated plywood with a center hole cut out and galvanized screen wire fastened over the hole is the divider. It's fastened to a cleat on the underside of the center top piece which is anchored solidly to the tank top. Lids on both sides are hinged to the center strip. This works quite well, but you can improve the keeping ability by adding an overflow drain tube and an intake attached to a garden hose. It doesn't take much, just a trickle of fresh water will maintain livelier bait. The tank should be placed in a cool dark spot in your garage or shed.

Several tactics can also help keep baits longer. First, remove all dead bait immediately. Check your tank morning and evening and remove any dead minnows. Limit handling of all bait as much as possible, and then handle them gently. Rock salt (approximately 1½ cups per 26 gallons) can be added each time you fill the tank to help keep scales intact. Rinse agitator and tank thoroughly after each use to reduce harmful bacteria and algae. Minnows can be transported in minnow buckets, aerated minnow buckets or live wells. Aerated minnow buckets are the best choice.

Leeches

Walleye love leeches, especially lunker walleye. Normally, leeches must be purchased, but you can also collect leeches if they're in your area. Leeches feed on blood. Simply place a piece of bloody calf's liver in a minnow trap and place in a creek or lake. Do not confuse the blood-sucker or creek leech with a bait leech. Walleye do not particularly like blood sucker leeches. To tell the difference, place the leech in your hand. If it curls up when you touch it, it's commonly a bait leech. Bait leeches also feel solid to the touch. Blood suckers are soft and squishy feeling.

Purchased leeches normally come in several sizes; if you're pestered by panfish, use the jumbo size.

Leeches are easy to keep as they don't require aeration. Simply place them in a Styrofoam container, such as an old cooler, with cold water and keep the water changed often. You normally don't have to change the water but every couple of days, depending on temperature. Keep the container in a cool place. Keeping in an old refrigerator can extend the life of the bait.

Nightcrawlers

If there's a number one walleye bait, it's a nightcrawler. And, nightcrawlers are the number one bait for most of the year, except in really cold weather, when nightcrawlers tend to be sluggish. Nightcrawlers are available almost anywhere including many quick-stop stations and even in grocery stores in some locales. But there are crawlers and there are crawlers. The best crawlers are fat and sassy. Ordinary garden worms can also be used, but they're smaller and usually not as "active" in attracting walleye.

You can also collect your own crawlers. The best time is after a long, soaking nighttime rain. As the rain saturates the soil, it drives the crawlers up to the surface. You can oftentimes simply pick a good number off your driveway, on the sidewalks, and I sometimes even find them in my garage. If the rain stops in the night, you can quite often collect nightcrawlers with a flashlight with a red lens in short-cropped grass areas. Folks have invented many different tactics and products for collecting worms. Some utilize a battery-powered unit that stimulates worms and drives them to the surface. One old-fashioned method is "fiddling up" worms. A notched stick is driven into the ground and another stick rubbed up and down the notches to create a vibration to bring worms to the surface. A potato fork driven into the ground and struck with another object also sometimes works.

Keeping earthworms is fairly easy, and growing a supply is also fairly easy. Growing nightcrawlers takes a bit more effort, but keeping them is, again, fairly easy. Simply keep them in a Styrofoam box in a refrigerator. You can keep a good quantity in this manner, and when you head to the lake simply take a small Styrofoam cooler with a day's supply. A small ice pack in the cooler will help keep the worms throughout the day, especially if the day is hot. Some anglers like to condition their worms the night before by placing them between ice-cold layers of wet newspaper, or you can simply toss them in a container of ice water the night before. They will be fat and wiggly.

You can easily raise garden worms, or purchased "red wigglers," but raising nightcrawlers takes a great deal more expertise and work. You'll need a container to hold the worms (a large old cooler is a good choice), but you must drill a few small holes in the top for ventilation. Fill

Earthworms and nightcrawlers can be kept using a variety of products available.

the container with a good garden soil that is not sandy. Thoroughly mix in one cup of dry dog food and sprinkle about a quart of water over the soil. Place twenty-five to fifty earthworms on top of the soil. Dampen a couple of sheets of newspaper and place over the worms.

Place the worm box in a cool part of your basement, away from the furnace, but where the temperature will stay 60 to 75 degrees Fahrenheit. Temperature is very important. If the temperature rises much above 70 degrees, the worms may die; if the temperature drops below 60 degrees, reproduction may be slowed. Use an inexpensive thermometer to monitor the soil temperature.

Inspect your worm box once a week. If the surface is dry add a little water, but don't overwater. If the soil is muddy, you're overfeeding and overwatering. About every three weeks remove the top two or three inches of soil and mix in one-half cup of dry dog food. Dump the remainder of the soil out and check on your worm "herd." Place the newly fed soil in the bottom of the container and replace the rest of the soil and the worms. In six to eight weeks you should have a new crop of worms. And if you're a good worm farmer, you can expect from seven hundred to a thousand worms.

Raising nightcrawlers, however, is a bit trickier. They require a bedding tempera-

A variety of bait-gathering products are available.

ture of 40 to 50 degrees Fahrenheit. You can keep a large supply, however, over a long period of time if you have a refrigerator and a worm box that fits inside it. Quite frankly, if you're going to try raising nightcrawlers, your best bet is the Magic Products worm bedding.

ABOUT THE AUTHOR

Monte Burch grew up fishing the Osage River in central Missouri for walleye and now fishes across the country for "old marble eyes." He lives near and fishes three major reservoirs well known for walleye. Monte has covered numerous professional walleye tournaments and is a regular contributor to major national magazines and the author of numerous books.

Professional walleye anglers Mike McClelland, Mike Theyerl, Gary Parsons, and Ralph Brunner have helped contribute information for this book.

NOTES

NOTES

NOTES